THE GOLDEN KEY

Emmet Fox

Narrated by Yousell Reyes

Copyright © 2023 YRV Publishing
All rights reserved.

CONTENTS

EDITOR'S PREFACE........................4

PREFACE...6

THE GOLDEN KEY 8

ABOUT THE AUTHOR.................18

ABOUT THE EDITOR 20

EDITOR'S PREFACE

I present this edition of "The Golden Key" by Emmet Fox with great pleasure and a sense of responsibility. This timeless classic has touched the lives of countless individuals, providing them with a simple yet powerful method to overcome life's challenges and achieve harmony and happiness.

In today's fast-paced, technology-driven world, it is more important than ever to find solace and guidance in the spiritual teachings that have withstood the test of time. "The Golden Key" offers just that, focusing on the power of scientific prayer and unwavering faith in the omnipotent presence of God. Emmet Fox's words remind us that the ultimate solution to our problems lies within ourselves through our connection with the divine.

The straightforward teachings of these pages may initially appear misleading, but if applied, they can significantly influence your existence. By employing the golden key in the face of every obstacle, you will uncover the transformative potential of shifting your focus from the issue at hand to God.

May "The Golden Key" serve as a constant companion on your spiritual journey, unlocking the door to inner peace, harmony, and a life filled with God's presence.

I wish you a transformative experience and a beautiful life!

Yousell Reyes
Editor

PREFACE

Striving for brevity and conciseness, I have refined the message for this edition. Ideally, I would have simplified it even further into just a few lines.

This work is not meant to be a step-by-step manual; it is designed to serve as a practical guide that aids you in dealing with difficult circumstances.

While studying and research have their merits, they are often insufficient when it comes to disentangling oneself from a problematic situation. Engaging in practical exercises to enhance your own consciousness can prove more effective. A typical error individuals make when encountering adversity is skimming through numerous books without making any real headway. This approach merely causes us to revisit the issue and fret about the consequences.

To overcome life's challenges, read The Golden Key multiple times and follow its instructions diligently. Then, with persistence, you CAN surmount any obstacles you meet.

Emmet Fox

THE GOLDEN KEY

SCIENTIFIC PRAYER will empower you (or anyone else) to overcome any difficulty; this is the golden key to harmony and happiness.

For those unfamiliar with the most potent POWER that exists, this may seem like a bold claim. However, a fair trial is all it takes to prove, without a shadow of a doubt, that it works. You don't need to rely on anyone's word, and you shouldn't. Try it for yourself, and you will see.

God is omnipotent, and as we are made in God's image and likeness, we have dominion over all things. This teaching is intended to be taken literally at face value. Harnessing this power is not an exclusive privilege of mystics or saints, as often assumed, or highly trained practitioners. Everyone has this ability.

Whoever you are, wherever you may be, the golden key to harmony is now in your hands; this is because, in scientific prayer, it is God who works, not you. Thus, your specific limitations or weaknesses are outside the process.

You are the sole channel through which divine action occurs, and your treatment involves getting out of the way.

Even beginners often achieve astonishing results the first time, as having an open mind and enough faith to try the experiment are essential. Beyond that, one's religious beliefs or lack thereof can vary.

As for the actual working method, like all fundamental things, it is the epitome of simplicity. All you need to do is this: STOP THINKING ABOUT THE DIFFICULTY, WHATEVER IT MAY BE, AND THINK ABOUT GOD; this is the complete rule, and if you only do this, the problem, whatever it may be, will vanish.

It doesn't matter what type of difficulty it is. It can be big or small, involving health, finances, a lawsuit, a quarrel, an accident, or anything imaginable. Whatever it is, STOP THINKING ABOUT IT AND THINK ABOUT GOD. That's all you need to do.

Could it be any more uncomplicated? God has seemingly designed this method with the utmost simplicity in mind, and it consistently proves effective when given a genuine opportunity. Do not try to form an image of God, which is impossible. Work by rehearsing anything or everything you know about God. God is wisdom, truth, and inconceivable love. God is present everywhere, possesses infinite power, and knows everything. No matter how well you think you understand these things, go over them repeatedly.

Remember: God is not a Super-Being somewhere in the sky. God is Spirit, always within and around you. God is the very essence of your True Self. God is the answer to every apparent problem.

You must STOP dwelling on the problem, whatever it may be. The rule is to think only of God. When you focus on your challenges, your thoughts drift away from God.

Continually looking over your shoulder to see how things are going is destructive, as it shows that your attention is on the issue rather than on God. You must THINK ABOUT GOD, nothing else.

Your aim is to expel the idea of the difficulty from your consciousness, at least briefly, by replacing it with the thought of God; this is the essence of the entire matter. If you can become so absorbed in contemplating the spiritual world that you forget about the problem for a moment, you will find yourself safe and comfortably out of the difficulty; your demonstration is made.

To apply the "golden key" to a problematic person or challenging situation, think: "Now I am going to use the 'golden key' on John or Mary or that threatening menace," then proceed to remove all thoughts of John or Mary or the danger from your mind, replacing them with thoughts of God.

When working in this manner with a person, you are not trying to influence their behavior in any way except to prevent them from hurting or bothering you, and you are doing them nothing but good. From then on, they will be, to some extent, a better, wiser, and more spiritual person simply because you have given them the "golden key." A pending lawsuit or another difficulty will likely fade harmlessly away without reaching a crisis, with justice being done to all parties involved.

Suppose you can do this rapidly. In that case, you may repeat the operation several times a day, with intervals in between. Ensure, however, that each time you have done it, you stop thinking about the matter until the next time; this is crucial.

We have said that the golden key is simple, and it is, but of course, it can be challenging to use. If you are extremely frightened or worried, it may be difficult to divert your thoughts from material things. Instead, constantly repeat an affirmation of absolute Truth, such as: "There is no power but God; I AM the child of God, filled and surrounded by God's perfect peace; God is love. God is guiding me now", or perhaps best and simplest of all, "God is with me," no matter how mechanical or clichéd it may seem.

You will soon discover that the treatment has begun to "take effect" and that your mind is clearing. Do not struggle; be quiet but insistent. Every time you find your attention wandering, bring it back to God.

Do not try to think in advance about the solution to your difficulty; this is called "outlining" and will only delay the demonstration. Instead, leave the matter of ways and means to God. You want to get out of your difficulty; that is enough. Just do your part, and God will never fail to do God's part.

"Whoever calls on the name of the Lord shall be saved." (Acts 2:21)

FIN

ABOUT THE AUTHOR

Emmet Fox was an influential Irish-born author and spiritual lecturer, born in 1886 and died in 1951. He was known for his teachings about New Age and metaphysics, based on the belief in the power of thought and mind to transform reality. Fox focused his teachings on the Bible and the symbolic interpretation of its texts. He is the author of numerous books, being "The Sermon on the Mount" and "The Golden Key" two of his most outstanding works. His ideas influenced the New Thought movement and the formation of Alcoholics Anonymous.

Emmet Fox was also known for his meditation practices and positive affirmations. Through his talks and writings, he taught his followers to focus on the power of the mind to achieve prosperity, health, and peace of mind. Fox believed strongly in the connection between mind, body, and spirit, and in the ability of every individual to overcome obstacles and achieve their goals using the force of thought. His teachings emphasized the importance of prayer and connection with God, whom he called the "Presence," as the origin of all power and wisdom. Fox also focused on the importance of forgiving and loving others, as well as the need to have constructive, positive thoughts and actions.

ABOUT THE EDITOR

Yousell Reyes, a native of Puerto Rico, is a published author and translator. He has published several books that aim to empower and inspire people to reach their full potential. In addition, Yousell spends a significant amount of time updating and translating ancient works, making them more accessible to a modern audience.

As a father of two, Yousell values family time and prioritizes balancing his passion for writing and translating with spending quality time with loved ones. One of his favorite pastimes is watching movies with your kids and enjoying a bowl of popcorn. He believes that moments shared with family are crucial for personal growth and development.

Yousell's goal is to make a positive impact on the lives of others and help them achieve success in their personal and professional lives. Through his writings and translations, he hopes to empower people to believe in themselves and pursue their dreams.

If you enjoyed this book and received value from it in any way, I would like to ask you a favor: Would you be so kind as to leave a review of this book on Amazon/Kindle? Thank you!

THE GOLDEN KEY

NOTES:

Printed in Great Britain
by Amazon